themooddiary

For Diane,
a very special sister

....

This edition published in Great Britain in 2020
by Eddison Books Limited
www.eddisonbooks.com

Text and illustrations copyright © Andrea Harrn 2020
Design © Eddison Books Limited 2020

Illustrations by Stacey Siddons

British Library Cataloguing-in-Publication data available on request.

ISBN 978-1-85906-456-6

1 3 5 7 9 10 8 6 4 2

Printed in Europe

PLEASE NOTE
The author and publisher cannot accept any responsibility for misadventure resulting from the practice of any
of the principles and techniques set out in this book. This book is not intended as guidance for the treatment of
serious mental and/or physical health problems; please take note of any cautionary advice given, and refer to a
medical professional if you are in any doubt about any aspect of your condition.

themooddiary

a 4-week plan to track your emotions and lifestyle

andrea harrn

e

Eddison Books Ltd

CONTENTS

Preface

As a psychotherapist with 20 years' experience, I often recommend my clients keep weekly diary sheets to record patterns of moods, emotions, stress anxiety, depression, sleep, food and triggers to addictions. This helps people gain better perspective on their lives to see if and where change needs to happen. I am neither a scientist nor an expert on physical exercise, human anatomy, sleep or nutrition, but over the years I have seen remarkable improvements in people's lives when taking a more solution-focused approach that includes these elements. I also want to say at this point that if you are experiencing mental health problems, mood disorders, personality disorders or other problematic issues, I am not suggesting that changing thoughts and behaviours will take away or fix your problems. It's not that simple, but I'm sure you know that already. What I'm sharing with you in this book is a snapshot, easy-to-read, common-sense guide to healthy living, which I invite you to consider for positive change.

The approach used in this diary is very much holistic, looking at the 'whole' with a focus on CBT (cognitive behavioural therapy) to help you challenge any negative fixed thoughts or opinions to develop a positive growth mindset. Positive thinking will not change situations, but will help you to realize that you will be OK no matter what. The diary will help you not only get in touch with your feelings and release them in a cathartic way, but also start the process of self-examination – into the way you think, perceive and talk (to yourself and others) about your life. CBT specifically looks at rational versus irrational thinking, belief systems, resultant feelings and behaviour. It might be a challenge, but if you are willing to take it onboard and work with it, CBT can rewire your mental patterns (neurotransmitters – brain messengers), which can create new neural pathways in your brain to improve the way you feel. If your mind was your mobile phone, you wouldn't hesitate to constantly update it for smooth running. In fact, you would probably replace it for the latest model. I'm not saying you need a brain transplant here, just a few simple updates to replace thoughts that no longer serve you, while keeping those that do.

This book is a 4-week journey into your life. I have found using diaries for this specific length of time to be motivating, fun and easy to complete, giving sufficient time to bring powerful learning and change without becoming a chore.

Introduction

Managing emotions is a challenge that we all face at different points in our lives. For some this is easy, but for those with anxiety disorders, mood disorders, personality disorders, depression or other mental health issues, it can be a lot harder.

It is often not the events in our lives, but our perceptions of them and our strategies for coping when things feel difficult that cause us problems. Some people tune out feelings altogether, while others become overwhelmed. We are all different and there is no right or wrong way for you to feel or behave. Sometimes we just don't know what is right for us because we can become confused in self-doubt and negativity, which is why mood journals, trackers and diaries are great tools to help us understand ourselves.

Widely recommended by many counsellors and therapists, a mood diary is a beneficial and effective self-management tool for positive change. Whether you are struggling to manage your moods, have a mental health diagnosis or are simply going through a difficult time, this book will help you to educate yourself, take control and make positive changes to help you lead a healthier, happier life. This process can also be much easier and more fun than you think; once you get started you will find it enjoyable, informative and motivating.

Whatever you have been told in the past about you, your moods, personality or your diagnoses, be prepared to have a new and open view of yourself. Don't hold yourself back by limiting self-belief of what is or is not possible. Make a decision to enter into this 4-week period with commitment and interest. Don't be stuck on the outcome. Embrace the journey.

HOW DOES IT WORK?

For just a few minutes each day, writing in your diary will be a powerful and effective way to monitor your life. There are daily entries to complete, freewriting pages, CBT (cognitive behavioural therapy) worksheets, weekly evaluations and goal planners. You are encouraged to:

1 Look at your mood, food, exercise, pain levels, sleep quality or other factors and rate your energy level using a score of 1–10

2 Write down how each day has panned out for you, taking account of the positives as well as the negatives

3 Complete themed CBT worksheets to change your mindset

4 Use the freewriting pages twice per week to release thoughts and feelings and be more self-reflective

5 Fill out a weekly evaluation to check your progress, identify themes and learn

6 Plan positive goals for the following week

HOW CAN THE DIARY HELP ME?

The diary gives you an opportunity to step back from yourself and see things as they truly are. It can be used alone or in conjunction with counselling. It is your diary to keep as confidential as you choose. It will help you to:

▶ See patterns and identify themes that emerge

▶ Identify triggers or other negative influences that may be holding you back from living a life free of stress, anxiety, conflict or depression

▶ Get to the bottom of what bothers you most

▶ Connect to your deepest emotions and feelings without judgement.

▶ Express yourself, in your own way, using your own style, words and language, which is therapy in itself

▶ Develop strategies, goals and routine for wellness and positivity using a CBT approach

▶ See how changing your mindset can change your life

In this book, you will be invited to fill out CBT worksheets each week. The following page shows a typical CBT worksheet using the example of a job interview. The situation itself is not the problem, it's how we think about it that makes it so. CBT looks at negative thoughts and resultant emotion. It then rates the strength of belief in each thought and the intensity of each emotion using a percentage scale of 1–100. Whatever you tell yourself will be felt as a truth. Changing to more helpful thinking will change the emotional outcome. The emotion in the right-hand column relate to each separate thought in the left-hand column.

Throughout the diary, there is also tips, advice and guidance to help you feel better and more positive about the future. Write freely and honestly in your own style, using the questions for self-inquiry as a guide. Remember to notice what went well each day so you can list your daily gratitudes and practice the power of positive affirmations to increase your feeling of contentment.

So are you feeling excited,
energized and motivated to start?
Let's go…

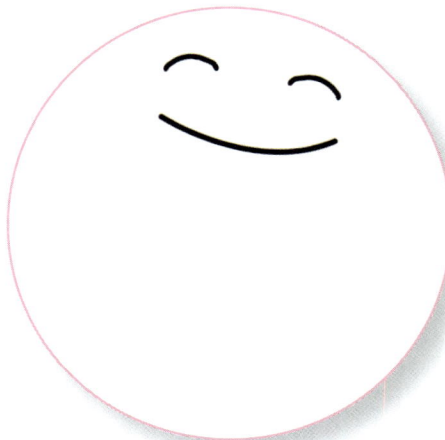

SAMPLE CBT WORKSHEET

SITUATION	NEGATIVE THOUGHTS Strength of belief (1–100%)	NEGATIVE EMOTIONS Intensity of emotion (1–100%)
Going for a job interview	I won't be able to do it (50%)	Worry (80%)
	They won't like me (20%)	Anxiety (85%)
	I'm hopeless at interviews (70%)	Powerless (75%)
	I'll never get this (80%)	Disappointed (75%)
	I can't communicate (10%)	Sad (70%)

SAME SITUATION	POSITIVE THOUGHTS Strength of belief (1–100%)	POSITIVE EMOTIONS Intensity of emotion (1–100%)
	I can see what the job entails (100%)	Interested (80%)
	I'm hardworking and keen (90%)	Hopeful (90%)
	I have some relevant experience (100%)	Proud (90%)
	I'll do my best (100%)	Determined (100%)
	I have a good chance of getting this (50%)	Motivated (100%)
	I can communicate well and I will ask lots of questions (80%)	Happy (100%)

Your moods

According to science, happiness is the presence of four primary feel-good chemicals in the brain: dopamine, serotonin, endorphins and oxytocin. All of which can be produced naturally though healthy eating, regular exercise and a positive mindset. Sounds simple doesn't it? You and I know that really it isn't simple at all: if it was, then everyone would be happy most of the time. But that's not real life.

There are many ways to describe happiness but I like to think of it as inner peace, contentment, joy, acceptance and gratitude. Everyone deserves to be happy, it does not depend on who you are or what you have achieved. What does happiness mean to you?

We all experience moods and emotions that fluctuate and change, which makes life interesting as well as challenging. Hormones can have a huge effect on our emotions at different stages of life and many of us will also experience anxiety and depression. For many people, riding the roller coaster of emotions can feel so hard to handle. If your life feels out of control and this has been a long-term pattern for you, an assessment by a qualified professional can be helpful in diagnosing and finding the right treatments. Then there are the sensitive types: the empaths, the creatives, the strong right-brainers and the co-dependents. They feel so deeply emotional when faced with conflict or abuse that it can be hard to think straight, cope or put necessary boundaries in place.

Communicating with friends and/or family is an effective way to reduce and manage difficult emotions. However, when people struggle to talk, it can manifest in unhealthy coping mechanisms, like addictions to drugs or alcohol or other self-harming behaviours. We are all entitled to our feelings and not wrong or unworthy for having them.

So why is it that some people cope better than others when life doesn't run smoothly? Those who cope best are generally the people who know that life does not run smoothly and are not surprised by that fact. They don't have overly high or unrealistic expectations of themselves or others, are more able to accept circumstances, be more resilient to change and can forgive and move on more easily (rather than holding on to anger and resentment), being more in the flow, less controlling and rigid.

When I ask clients about their goals for therapy the answers are fairly similar:
* To reduce stress, anxiety and panic attacks
* To work on anger management

* To resolve issues (childhood, trust, betrayal, conflict)
* To not be depressed
* To manage feelings and behaviours
* To get back to their old self
* To feel happy within

Happiness and peace of mind is what most people strive for. It's the pot of gold at the end of the rainbow, but not a destination in itself. Life is not a straight road, more a series of ups and downs, detours and backtracks, pleasure and pain. Furthermore, we are not all born equal or raised in perfect environments. Early experience plays a large part in later emotional resilience. To thrive, certain conditions need to be in place. According to American psychologist Maslow, these conditions are food, warmth, sleep, safety and security (the physiological needs) and to feel loved and cared for, initially by parents or primary caregivers and then as adults in relationships with partners or friends (the psychological needs). Without these we can be left feeling insecure, unworthy and mistrusting. Poverty, addiction and long-term mental health conditions can seriously affect a family's ability to provide these key conditions. Patterns are then repeated through generations, which means that some people may be more prone than others to experience mental health issues. It's the nature/nurture debate! Please don't blame yourself for your situation: it is not your fault. If your joy and innocence was hijacked as a child, maybe it's time to think about meeting your own needs from now on, creating your own security, reclaiming happiness and finding your present-day 'self' – a self that doesn't need validation and approval from others.

We can neither control nor be responsible for the thoughts, opinions and actions of others. Our worth doesn't depend on how we are judged or perceived by them. It depends on how we value ourselves. If you are forever reacting you are not taking control. Now is the time to change your story.

TIPS:

▶ Begin each day with a breathing meditation to feel relaxed and calm
▶ Set your intention for the day (today I will feel calm or today I will finish X)
▶ Practice mindfulness regularly
▶ See opportunities in every moment
▶ Find joy and happiness in small things
▶ Detach from the judgements of others
▶ Practice the art of non-reaction
▶ Resolve to be strong in your actions, not weak in your reactions
▶ Write a gratitude list each day

Naming your emotions

It is quite normal for moods and emotions to change throughout the day. We can wake up feeling one way and 2 hours later feel different, depending on circumstances: quality of sleep, weather, traffic, relationships, work deadlines, expectations of ourselves, exams… The list is endless. We cannot always feel high but neither do we want to feel low for extended periods. Sometimes it can be hard to find the right words to define exactly how we feel. Many people tend to lump feelings and emotions into good or bad:

Meh, down, fed up vs great, buzzing, fine.

But what about the in-between states: neither very happy nor very sad? Being able to identify the emotion you are feeling is a great way to learn to master it. Think about how it feels physically as well as mentally. Does it feel nice and warm or cold and tense? Can you cope with it? Do you want to change it or enjoy it? There are so many words to label feelings that it is hard to know where to start. Let's look at them in terms of core emotions with a wide range of emotional labels that fall within. Some examples follow on the next page.

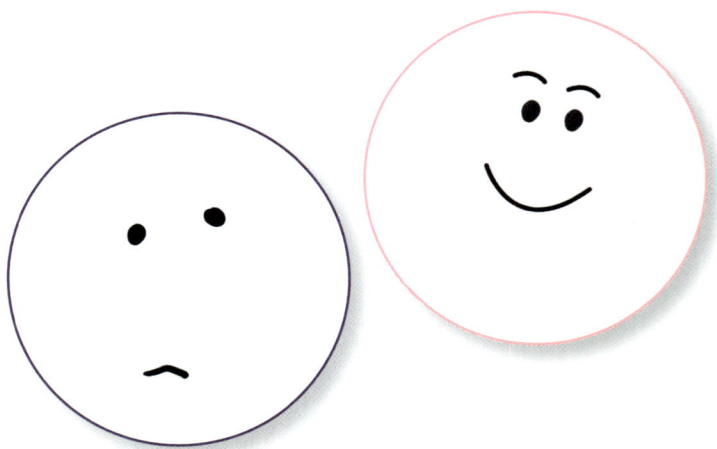

CORE EMOTION	EMOTIONAL LABELS
Anger	Rage, annoyed, bitter, resentful, hateful, destructive, frustrated, seething
Sadness	Depressed, hurt, disappointed, despairing, unhappy, miserable, lonely, despondent, disheartened, gloomy, miserable, confused
Depression	Tired, exhausted, lethargic, bored, complacent, indifferent, ambivalent, disinterested, confused, suicidal
Shame	Self-loathing, guilty, embarrassed, afraid, humiliated, worthless, regretful, sorry
Stress	Panic, anxiety, worry, dread, nervous, overwhelmed, undervalued, confused
Fear	Anxiety, dread, scared, terrified, paranoid, uneasy, nervous, panic, tensed, afraid
Disgust	Insulted, offended, disliking, intolerant, repulsed, sickened, wary, self-loathing
Rejection	Neglected, abandoned, isolated, lonely, insecure, worthless, rejected
Jealousy	Envious, mistrustful, greedy, vengeful, unhappy, afraid
Grief	Waves of shock, traumatised, loss, numb, lonely, angry, irrational, anxious, exhausted, jealous, frustrated, denial, guilty, rejected, depressed, indecisive, lost, dependent (not an exhaustive list)
Love	Attached, attracted, belonging, caring, empathic, compassionate, devoted, passionate, protective, respectful, vulnerable, hopeful
Happiness	Joyful, optimistic, hopeful, motivated, inspired, determined, proud, confident, excited
Blessed	Accepting, forgiving, contented, peaceful, joyful, compassionate, loving, grateful, free

Now let's look at some of the typical reasons people experience a range of emotions and some common thoughts people have. You will see how a positive situation does not always produce positive thoughts, especially where people are wary or mistrusting or believe that something will go wrong.

EMOTION	POSSIBLE REASONS WHY	COMMON THOUGHTS
ANGER	Not getting your own way Someone upset you	It's unfair They should or shouldn't have done X, Y or Z
SADNESS	Break up of a relationship Not feeling valued or appreciated	It must be my fault I'm not good enough
STRESS	Being overloaded at work Taking on too much responsibility	I can't say no It's down to me
DEPRESSION	Following on from stress or illness Not asking for help	I can't think straight I'm a burden to others

EMOTION	POSSIBLE REASONS WHY	COMMON THOUGHTS
FEAR	Belief that something bad will happen Expecting a bad reaction from others	I can't do that – it's dangerous There's no point in trying
DISGUST	Being around toxic people OCD – fear of contamination	They make me sick I'm disgusting
REJECTION	Partner cheats on you A loved one doesn't bother with you	What did I do wrong I'm worthless
SHAME	Doing something that goes against your values Being criticized or ridiculed	I'm an idiot I'm fat/ugly/stupid
JEALOUSY	Your ex has a new partner Someone else gets promoted	I've failed It should have been me

EMOTION	POSSIBLE REASONS WHY	COMMON THOUGHTS
GRIEF	A parent or close loved one dies	I should have done more
	A long-term relationship breaks up	I'll never love again
LOVE	Meeting your soulmate	This feels wonderful
	Finding happiness together	Too perfect – it won't last
HAPPINESS	Being around those you love	This feels good
	Counting your blessings	I'm so grateful for X, Y, Z
BLESSED	Being in the moment	Life is good
	Relaxing	I can't relax for too long
HOPEFUL	Belief that something good is going to happen	Life is good
	Opportunity arises for a life change	I'm just not sure

EMOTION	POSSIBLE REASONS WHY	COMMON THOUGHTS
BRAVE	Overcoming an illness Helping another person	I'm determined to beat this I can do this
VALUED	You had a productive work day You helped a friend who was in a difficult situation	I am proud of myself My efforts aren't always reciprocated
EXCITED	Going on a spontaneous holiday to a new destination Looking forward to moving house	I can't wait for this new experience I have so many ideas it's a bit overwhelming

Do you recognize some of these? Do you tend to think the worst about situations, even good ones? This is probably due to past experiences or conditioning. If you've been hurt or let down before, then you will be naturally wary of all situations, even positive ones: that is your protection. However, be careful not to let your past or your emotions define you. Feeling sad does not make you a sad person. What happened in the past is unlikely to be repeated, unless it is a situation over which you have no control. Learning about yourself, your experiences, your past and present actions, your reactions, your thoughts and your behaviours is the first step towards making empowering changes.

Understanding influences on your moods

The way we feel is dependent on so many factors, which could be physical, emotional or hormonal. Some factors may be out of our control, such as the behaviour and actions of others or a situation where we were not given a choice, like not getting a job we wanted or breaking up with a partner unexpectedly. There are, however, things we can change to make a positive difference to our moods. Let's look at those now:

THINKING

How we think about life, situations, ourselves and others has a huge impact on the way we feel, our physical reactions and our behaviour. One situation can be viewed in many different ways.

Many people with negative thinking patterns are more focused on the past or the future, beating themselves up for what they think they've done or haven't done or unnecessarily worrying and stressing about a future event.

Example: Being stuck in a traffic jam on your way to work.

NEGATIVE THOUGHTS	POSITIVE THOUGHTS
That's my day ruined	*It will soon pass*
I'm going to be late	*I'll listen to some music*
This is ridiculous	*It's one of those things*
⬇	⬇
Anxiety, huffing and puffing	**Feeling calm and relaxed**

EXERCISE

Physical activity releases endorphins into your system – the feelgood chemicals and natural pain blockers that can reduce stress, increase the release of sex hormones and bring feelings of euphoria. Other activities that release endorphins are eating your favourite food, music, receiving a massage or a session of acupuncture. Becoming physically stronger through exercise can increase your confidence and help you thrive.

FOOD

Food and nutrition play a key role in moods and overall wellness. Our relationship with food connects us to others and to nature, plants and animals and our attitude to food, cooking and eating plays a big part in what makes us whole as human beings, mentally, emotionally, physically and spiritually. Eating well means taking responsibility for what we put into our bodies. We can choose to honour and love ourselves by taking time to organize and prepare a balanced meal or we can take the easy option and eat ready-made, processed foods or a takeaway. Society these days seems to revolve around fast food that is cheap and easy rather than healthy food, which can take more time to prepare and, sadly, often costs more. In reality, the cost of not eating a healthy diet is felt in so many other ways than just our pockets. We need to alter our attitude to food: to be aware of climate change, to eat less red meat and to reduce our carbon footprint. Poor eating habits can develop over a lifetime, but it is never too late to change habits for the better. Try to develop a conscious awareness of when, what and how you are eating. Improving your diet will help your energy levels, your clarity of thinking and your overall mood.

Serotonin and dopamine are two of the four primary feelgood, happy-brain chemical messengers that are naturally produced by eating the right foods. Serotonin helps regulate moods, social behaviours, aids appetite and digestion and improves sleep and sexual desire, while dopamine is involved in reward, motivation, memory and attention. Often GPs prescribe SSRIs (antidepressants) to increase Serotonin but you can increase it yourself by eating foods containing tyrosine, like eggs, cheese, pineapple, tofu, salmon, nuts, seeds, turkey and spinach. Dopamine can be increased by eating almonds, bananas, eggs, beans, fish and chicken.

SLEEP

Many people with anxiety also suffer from sleep deprivation, and people with chronic insomnia can go on to suffer anxiety. It can become a negative cycle. Lack of sleep affects how we function throughout the day and can then lead to further worry and anxiety before bedtime. Because we are all unique, the amount of sleep we need will differ. The average sleep needed is 7–9 hours, but some people survive on far less. Teenagers need more (8–10 hours) and often struggle with changing biological sleep patterns shifting towards later sleep and wake-up times. What matters most is the number of hours that you need to feel ready for the day. Sleep is the time that we can fully rest and restore our bodies.

Lack of a good night's sleep can affect our energy levels, moods, memory, concentration and focus. This can have a knock-on effect at work and in relationships, which puts us at risk of stress and anxiety. When we are exhausted, we can feel demotivated, so exercise and new challenges may feel harder to start. A good night's sleep puts us in the game, ready for action and ready for the day.

PHYSICAL HEALTH

The link between physical health and mood is strong. People that experience health problems also often experience stress and long bouts of depression. It can be hard when you hear from specialists that your health problem may be stress related, especially when the pain has a physical diagnosis. The problem is that health problems causes stress and worry, which in turn causes tension in the body, exacerbating any physical symptoms. So what might start out as physical, ends up becoming emotional. It's very upsetting and debilitating, especially when nothing specific shows up on X-rays or other tests.

Non-specific health problems and pain are difficult to make sense of, and because time and energy is often spent waiting for appointments and answers or cures, that often holds people back from self-healing or finding alternative ways to feel better.

It is hard to break the cycle of pain, no energy and no action.

SOCIAL MEDIA

Ongoing research into social media and mental wellbeing consistently shows links between heavy use and poorer mental health. Regular posting, sharing, scrolling, swiping, liking, commenting and messaging is now a daily habit for many people. While it can be a positive tool for growth and learning, being glued to devices can have a bad effect on moods. Too much use also links to lack of physical movement and real-time social interactions. Meeting up with friends is a far healthier and fun way to live life.

Do you think of social media as a positive influence on your life or do you see it as an addiction, something that you need to do even though your intuition tells you it's bad for you? Perhaps you don't even remember a time without it.

Last year at a festival where I was leading workshops I had the pleasure to meet a group of six young teenagers who came up to me and asked if I would please look after their mobile phones. I was naturally intrigued to know why. They said that they had been talking about how they were at this amazing place and yet for most of the time they were staring at their screens. I asked them what they thought about social media, and here are some of their comments:

Wish it had never been invented
Feel stressed and anxious
If you post and no one likes it, you feel bad
You start to think everyone is having a better time than you
You're not even yourself on there – it's false

Can you relate to this? Think about how much time you spend on social media. Does it start when you wake up? How many friends do you have? What kind of friendships are they?

LOVE AND RELATIONSHIPS

Giving love and being loved are central to human connection and happiness. Love comes in many forms: in friendships, in the arts, in universal connectedness, in nature with pets and other animals, and, of course, in relationships. Being kind, loving and friendly to others is a good way to feel more happiness inside and can make a difference to their wellbeing at the same time. A smile can go a long way!

It is important to choose, as much as possible, to have positive relationships in our lives that support and nurture us. A lot of anxiety and worry happens when we find ourselves in dysfunctional relationships that are toxic, confusing, disappointing or abusive.

USEFUL RELATIONSHIP TIPS:
▶ Be assertive in communication
▶ State your thoughts and feelings using 'I' statements, such as 'I felt hurt when you said X, Y or Z' or 'I would like it if we could do X, Y or Z'
▶ Avoid accusations that can be seen as an attack and cause defensiveness in others, such as 'You did This or That'
▶ Respect that other people have a right to their own opinion, as do you
▶ Learn to like, love and accept yourself for who you are
▶ Listen to your intuition
▶ Know your worth – don't accept second best
▶ If someone causes you anxiety, stress, hurt and unhappiness, let them know – give them a chance to change
▶ If things don't improve, learn to detach and choose to avoid them
▶ Don't let someone else's behaviour steal your joy
▶ Know that you are not responsible for others' behaviour, thoughts, feelings, happiness and wellbeing

This can be with family, friends or partners. It is even harder to understand if you have grown up in an environment where conflict is not the norm. It is perfectly acceptable to have disagreements and different opinions to others, and it is helpful to honestly express them. However, when you are an open book, it can be hard to be faced with others that are not. Or perhaps you find it hard to say how you feel. There are many reasons people keep quiet, such as fear of conflict, worry about judgement (for self-protection),

Negative relationships include:
* Ongoing and persistent conflict
* Controlling partners
* People who don't have your back
* Toxic, manipulative behaviour
* Passive-aggressive or narcissistic behaviour
* People that put you down
* People that don't accept or value you for who you are
* People that always need to be right
* Poor boundaries
* Poor communication

This can lead to:
* Fear of communication
* Fear of response
* Anxiety and worry
* Doubting yourself
* Low self-esteem
* Poor sense of self-respect and worth

Positive relationships include:
* Trust and love
* Being able to communicate honestly without fear of negative reaction
* Not feeling the need to compare or compete
* Being yourself without feeling judged
* Acceptance of self and others' thoughts and opinions
* Strong boundaries
* Space for forgiveness

This will lead to:
* Confidence
* Motivation
* Peace of mind
* Empathy and self-compassion
* Self-respect
* Feelings of security

thinking you will not be properly heard, feeling you have no voice or not really knowing what you think. And then there are underlying reasons, such as previous experience of being hurt, wounded and abused, being bullied in the past or low self-esteem. It's complicated!

LOW SELF-ESTEEM

Self-esteem is the way you think, feel and value yourself. People with low self-esteem tend to see themselves as unworthy and that their opinions and ideas don't matter. Low self-esteem is characterized by: lack of confidence; low expectations fuelled by lack of belief in yourself and your abilities; or feeling bad or disgusted with who you are. It can also include: having judgemental and critical thoughts towards yourself; labelling yourself in unhelpful ways; focusing on negatives; and finding it hard to accept compliments. People with low self-worth can be hypersensitive to perceived disapproval and criticism and often find ways to interpret situations and others' behaviour as evidence that they are inadequate or lacking in some way. Typically they can feel fear, anxiety, stress, shame, awkwardness, disappointment, indecisiveness and overall hopelessness and helplessness.

When your inner critic takes over, negative thoughts tend to focus on signs of rejection, abandonment, not being liked, not being good enough, disappointing others, being a burden and failing in some way. All or nothing thinking tends to take over:

I'm an idiot vs *I'm good at X and Y*

Signals can be misinterpreted quite easily when you see someone is annoyed or disapproving, even when it is not about you.

Example: You are upset about a friend's perceived behaviour towards you.

YOUR VERSION	REALITY
They don't really like me	They have their own problems
There's no point in being her friend	They have no idea they've upset you
I need to be wary	They are also feeling upset
She's got style, I'm a mess	You have your own style

When people find it hard to release anxious and upsetting thoughts it can feel like carrying around a heavy pressure cooker of emotions about to boil over or explode. Talking about feelings can be a huge relief and very helpful in gaining new perspectives. When that feels too hard to do, other unhealthy coping defence mechanisms can manifest, which over time develop into problems such as addictions, OCD or self-harm, and these symptoms then become viewed as the 'main' problem.

Rather than being hard on yourself for not meeting up to your own self-expectations, how about being kind and compassionate instead? After all, you are an imperfect human like the rest of us.

TIPS TO BOOST CONFIDENCE:

▶ Be yourself
▶ Trust yourself
▶ Listen to your intuition
▶ Talk honestly to friends and family about the way you feel
▶ Respect, honour and value yourself
▶ Make your own decisions about your life
▶ Be assertive about your needs
▶ Recognize your skills and strengths
▶ Stop listening to the inner voice that puts you down, judges and criticizes you. The voice that says: 'I'm stupid' or 'I'm worthless'
▶ Notice your inner qualities
▶ Be your own best friend
▶ Move on from difficult incidents without blame
▶ Find forgiveness

▶ Act in alignment with your own principles and moral code:
    Live and let live
    Bullying is wrong
    I don't need to behave badly just because someone else has
    I don't need to attend every argument – I can choose peace instead
▶ Be loving, kind and compassionate towards yourself and others
▶ Have fun and try not to take life too seriously
▶ Make your life count through meaningful actions:
    Volunteer for a charity
    Smile at a stranger
    Carry out random acts of kindness
▶ Write a daily gratitude list

Mental health conditions

People develop mental health issues for a variety of reasons – the cause is not exactly clear or precise, as we all have a unique life story. Let's now look at how to recognize some of the common mental health problems that affect people's moods:

STRESS

Stress often follows major life-changing events, such as death of a loved one, divorce or separation, personal injury or illness, long-term health conditions, marriage, having children, and also work-related problems such as unemployment, job insecurity, redundancy or bullying and overload.

Stress symptoms can include: racing thoughts; anxiety; panic attacks; worry; feeling on edge, irritable or annoyed; feeling overwhelmed; fear of something awful happening; sleep issues; change in appetite; trouble relaxing; difficulty concentrating. Stress can also create physical pain like headaches, back ache, IBS and other more serious health conditions.

ANXIETY

Some people have anxiety that is more pervasive and long term, such as general anxiety disorder (GAD) – which is an anxiety that switches from one thing to another (fear of flying, going up in lifts, for example) – or health anxiety (obsessive and compulsive worries about illness and disease).

DEPRESSION

Depression can happen for a number of reasons or for no reason at all, which makes it hard to make sense of; you might on the surface have everything to be happy about but still feel depressed. It often follows major stressful incidents but can also be influenced by genetics, family history, hormones or medical conditions. When life doesn't meet our needs to feel secure, loved and valued we begin to disconnect from 'living'. We all need purpose and meaning but so many of us are not truly fulfilled on a day-to-day basis, especially when we feel unappreciated and that we have no control over our lives. Try changing the word 'depressed' to 'deep rest' and see this as your spiritual awakening moment, your body giving you a sign to take time out and find a new path for yourself.

Depression symptoms can include: feeling heavy, hopeless, helpless, tired, a failure, a burden on others; lack of energy and motivation; difficulty concentrating; changes in speech; suicidal thoughts; finding it hard to see the light. It can feel like a struggle to get up each day, to eat, to sleep and to live.

BIPOLAR DISORDER (BD)

Bipolar disorder (BD) condition relates to emotional extremities – manic or hypomanic (highs) and depressive (lows) with mixed states in between. It can be very distressing and overwhelming to be uncontrollably excited and invincible one moment, leading to possible reckless behaviour, followed by feelings of shame, guilt and regret the next.

Symptoms include: unpredictability of mood; intense emotional pain; thoughts of self-harm or suicide; problems in relationships; disrupted eating and sleep patterns; feeling empty, exhausted or suicidal.

BORDERLINE PERSONALITY DISORDER (BPD)

People with BPD have an ongoing struggle to manage moods, emotions and behaviour. It is also very hard for others to understand. BPD involves a fear of abandonment, which often becomes a self-fulfilling prophecy when sufferers lash out at loved ones.

Symptoms include: low self-esteem; low self-confidence; anxiety; depression; feelings of loneliness and emptiness; impulsive, self-destructive and sometimes reckless behaviours; self-harm; explosive anger; extreme mood swings.

ADDICTIONS

Addiction is when a person feels unable to control their behaviour, such as with substance misuse, and becomes preoccupied with it, leading to life changing consequences, such as the loss of a job, loss of driving licence, getting in trouble with the police, loss of relationships and loss of access to children. It is a disease of the mind, body and soul. Some people that become addicts also have a history of dysfunctional, troubled childhoods, featuring emotional, physical and/or sexual abuse, violence and chaos. Alternatively, addiction can be caused by genetic factors like a family history of alcoholism or drug addiction. Not everyone that engages in unhelpful behaviours becomes addicted, but when using a substance to escape reality or mask emotional pain, it can become compulsive. Many addicts go through a cycle of addiction that leads to negative feelings such as anxiety, panic, fear, shame, guilt, disappointment, blame, loneliness and hopelessness.

Gambling, pornography and sex addition
With easy to access to gambling and pornography via the internet, where you can be anonymous, it is possible to not fully own your behaviour – it's almost like having an alter-ego that engages in bad and shameful acts. We all have a dark shadow side, which

helps us learn more about our identity and sense of self, but sadly internet technology knows how to find you and how to hook you, which is hard for many people to resist.

Codependency and Relationship Addiction
Codependents tend to fall for people that need 'fixing'. They have an over-exaggerated sense of responsibility for others, tend to give a lot more, hurt a lot more, care a lot more and, despite getting little back, will continue to make excuses rather than put boundaries in place, for fear of abandonment and rejection. Many codependents come from families where a parent or sibling had mental health issues or addictions. Many are also empaths and highly sensitive.

EATING DISORDERS

An unhealthy irrational attitude towards food and your body, includes anorexia, bulimia, BED (binge eating), BDD (body dysmorphia), or a combination of all of these disorders. Symptoms of eating disorders include:

* Being obsessed about keeping your weight as low as possible
* Not eating enough food (anorexia)
* Losing control of eating in a very short time and then throwing up (bulimia)
* Regularly losing control of eating large portions of food all at once (binging)

Other behaviours include: over-exercising; being obsessed with looking in the mirror; weighing yourself all the time; hiding food; and lying about your lifestyle, all of which can lead to feelings of anxiety, worry, fear, guilt and shame. It can also lead to avoidance of social gatherings for fear of losing control of eating or being judged by others. Longer term symptoms include problems with digestion, feeling physically tired, cold or dizzy, and not getting periods.

OBSESSIVE COMPULSIVE DISORDER (OCD)

OCD is an anxiety-related addictive disorder grounded in fear, which involves obsessions and compulsions.

Obsessive thinking could include:
* Ideas, images and intrusive thoughts that cause excess anxiety and worry that then lead to acting out (the compulsions)
* Horrific thoughts and mental images of causing harm and danger to others
* Sexual impulses that are clearly unwanted, disgusting and repulsive

When people have these awful thoughts they often need and seek reassurance that they will not act on them or harm others.

Compulsive behaviours, triggered by the obsessive thoughts might include:
* Checking doors, locks or windows

(fear of a security breach)

* Washing and cleaning (fear of contamination by germs, dirt, viruses)
* Ordering, counting and repeating (fear that if you don't, something bad will happen to a loved one), such as keeping clothes in a symmetrical way, or cans of food all facing the front, or going up and down the stairs three times before leaving the house
* Hoarding possessions or junk (fear and distress at the thought of letting go)

OCD is distressing, time-consuming and gets in the way of normal routines, relationships with others and daily functioning. It is often based on faulty beliefs, superstition, ritual and prayer. It can become a cycle of anxiety, acting out, slight relief, anxiety, more acting out and so on.

SELF-HARM

Also known as self-injury, self-harm includes cutting, scratching, skin ripping and picking, hair pulling, burning, biting or banging your body against a wall or other objects as a way of coping with intense emotional distress.

People who self-harm say it helps them to release emotional pain, to feel 'something'; it gives them a purpose, structure and control over themselves. The blood and injuries represent pain leaving the body. It distracts from emotional pain by replacing it with physical pain and can be a safer option than other reckless or dangerous behaviour (suicide attempts, for example). It is a form of self-punishment, striking inwards rather than reaching outwards. It can help to numb pain by releasing endorphins into the system.

In reality, self-harm does not solve any problems or take them away. It gives temporary relief but that may also be accompanied by feelings of shame. It also brings big concerns from loved ones. It may be that you don't think parents or friends will understand. You could be right, but you could be wrong. They may not understand how self-harm helps you, but they may be willing to listen and try to understand the reasons you are doing it. Perhaps in the past you have not felt heard or you think you don't matter. You do matter. If you cannot talk to others, please use this diary to write your deepest thoughts, fears and feelings so you can get them out of you. Words are not blood, but can be written in red.

MEDITATION AND MINDFULNESS TO HELP YOUR MOODS

Both meditation and mindfulness are scientifically proven ways to help manage emotions. There are various ways to meditate, but, essentially, it focuses on the breath and counting. Mindfulness is the practice of present moment awareness, via breathwork and observing our bodies, thoughts and feelings as well as our environment. Mindfulness is paying attention *on purpose*, not trying to change things but accepting what is.

Many of us spend our time focused either on the past or the future, paying very little attention to what is happening *now* in the present, which means that for much of the time, we may be unaware of our present experiences. Mindfulness helps us to accept the way things are for better or for worse and without judgement.

Try this mindfulness meditation exercise:

Sit in any comfortable position for meditation
Allow your body to settle
Feel a physical connection to where you are
Relax your head; feel your feet on the floor
Notice the breath enter and leave your body
Be aware of how your body moves with each breath
Relax your body with every breath
Notice any noises or sounds without judgement (just name them)
Be aware of the touch or feel of your hands in your lap
Breathe in and out at least five times, deepening on each breath
Notice any tension or feelings inside you — name them in a compassionate way
Feel the rise and fall of your breath
Notice the rise and fall of feelings
Breathe in calm and breathe out negativity
Notice the temperature around you; is it warm or cold?
Bring your attention to your thoughts
Breathe out any unhelpful thoughts (one at a time — watch them float away)
Repeat three times, breathing slowly and deeply
Feel your mind and body in a zone of peace and calm
When you feel ready, open your eyes, get up and carry on
See how long you can stay in this zone

Self-love and self-compassion

Sometimes it can be hard to even like yourself, let alone love yourself, especially when you have been hurt and let down by others. Rejection, abandonment, bullying or abuse can leave us feeling worthless and unloveable. The very suggestion that self-love is necessary to being loved is wrong.

Even if you don't love yourself, you are still worthy of being loved.

Rather than being hard on yourself, judgemental and critical, how about being more kind, appreciative, compassionate and caring? Treat yourself as you might treat others who are in need of love, support and encouragement. Listen to your own pain and suffering, and acknowledge that life might be hard at the moment. Open up your heart and show yourself loving kindness. Honour the little child inside you that needs and deserves to be loved. Be there for yourself

AFFIRMATIONS FOR SELF-COMPASSION:

I respect myself and my body

I honour myself

I will listen to my intuition (my inner guide)

I can take a step back where needed

I can choose who I spend time with

I am worthy of love

It's okay to say 'no'

I can set clear rules and boundaries for myself

I have the power to rise above situations

I can spend time alone if I choose

I can put myself first

I can relax

I can soothe my own emotions

I accept myself for who I am

I forgive myself and can choose to forgive others

It's okay to be vulnerable

It's okay to ask for help

It's okay to be me

and be gentle, especially when life gets tough. Stop fighting to prove a point or change others. Let go of pressure and high expectations on yourself or others to act or be a certain way; instead love, forgive and accept yourself. Stop apologizing for yourself, you don't have to be sorry for being you. Remove all masks of false self and allow yourself to be real and sometimes vulnerable. After all, you are a human being like the rest of us, with faults, imperfections, inconsistencies and weaknesses. Whatever has happened in the past cannot be changed. It's okay to be vulnerable – it does not make you weak or unattractive to others. It can, in fact, be a great way to make connections through empathy. Never be afraid to be open and honest about your struggles as much as your successes.

Remember, you are not responsible for the thoughts, feelings, actions and behaviour of others. Because someone behaved in a certain way towards you, it does not make it your fault. Furthermore, many of the messages about yourself that others give you are simply not true. The person you are may

have been shaped by others but the person you become can be shaped by you.

Life is not always fair
No-one is perfect
We cannot always be in control

Be mindful of your emotions in a kind way, think about what the emotion is trying to tell you. Accept the feeling but don't become the emotion. Feeling angry does not make you an angry person. It's just a temporary feeling that will pass. Claim the right to feel the way you do in a caring way and start to observe yourself as others see you, which will help you to gain clarity and perspective.

Don't change so people will like you; be yourself and the right people will love the real you.

Self-respect
Self-protect
Self-compassion
Self-care
Self-love

SELF-CARE – THE WELLNESS WHEEL

Now let's look at self-care and making the very most of *your* life. The mind does not exist in isolation to the rest of your body – it is a part of an interconnected physical, emotional and spiritual system. To thrive as individuals we need to feed our wellness 'plate' with all the right ingredients.

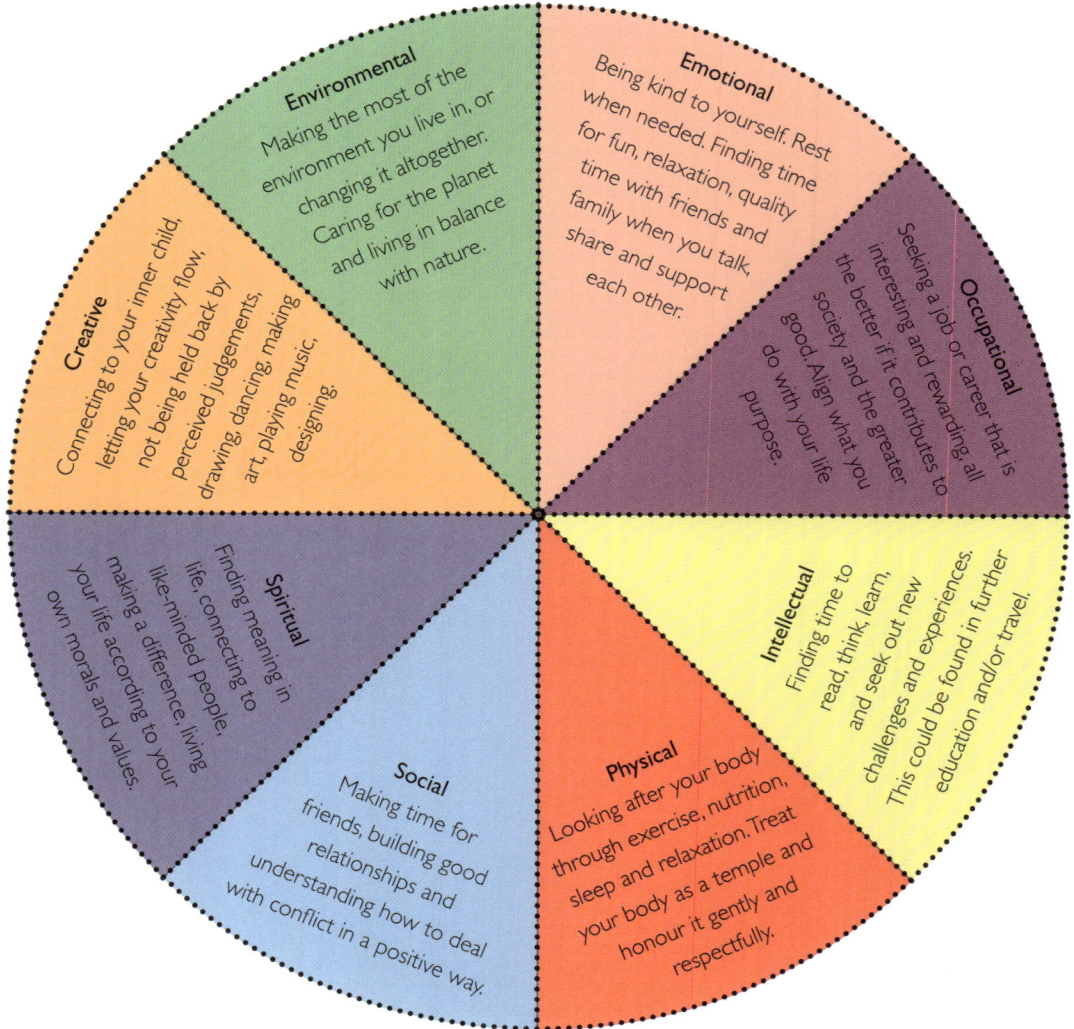

Environmental
Making the most of the environment you live in, or changing it altogether. Caring for the planet and living in balance with nature.

Emotional
Being kind to yourself. Rest when needed. Finding time for fun, relaxation, quality time with friends and family when you talk, share and support each other.

Occupational
Seeking a job or career that is interesting and rewarding all the better if it contributes to society and the greater good. Align what you do with your life purpose.

Creative
Connecting to your inner child, letting your creativity flow, not being held back by perceived judgements, drawing, dancing, making art, playing music, designing.

Intellectual
Finding time to read, think, learn, and seek out new challenges and experiences. This could be found in further education and/or travel.

Spiritual
Finding meaning in life, connecting to like-minded people, making a difference, living your life according to your own morals and values.

Social
Making time for friends, building good relationships and understanding how to deal with conflict in a positive way.

Physical
Looking after your body through exercise, nutrition, sleep and relaxation. Treat your body as a temple and honour it gently and respectfully.

Summary

So now you have read the introductory material, I look forward to being part of this 4-week self-development diary journey with you, where you can develop a new and empowering positive mental attitude.

Even if this feels like a challenge right now, because you are reading this diary, I'm going to assume that you would like at least to understand more about who you are, why you are the way you are and how to manage your moods and emotions. At the very least, you can end this 4-week period with more self-awareness than before. But I know you can go further than that. You can achieve far more than you think you can. You are capable of so many things. You have already achieved successes in life (perhaps you've forgotten). I believe in you. I'm with you.

Here are some affirmations for you:

I am willing to look at my life wholeheartedly
I will make powerful changes
I look forward to a bright future.

Let's do this…

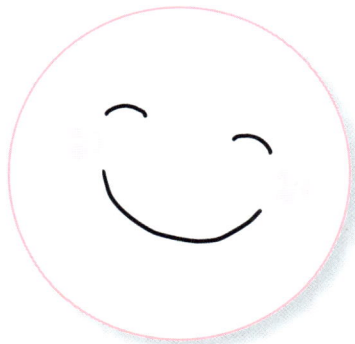

WEEK ONE

This first week is all about taking a good look at yourself and your life in this moment. You can log your overall mood for each day, quality of food and drink, amount of active exercise, overall energy level and quality of sleep. The 'other' section is yours to choose, as you will know what needs monitoring. Write freely and honestly in your own style.

The themed CBT worksheets for this week focus on thinking and how negative and positive thoughts can affect your emotions and behaviours. There are questions for self-inquiry as well as an opportunity write the things you are grateful for and a positive affirmation. Being grateful for even the smallest of joys at the end of each day will help you to focus on the whole (instead of the bad bits), rewire your brain to pay attention to the positives and increase your feeling of contentment, thereby improving your sleep quality. Some examples of positive affirmations are:

I can do this
I trust myself

Some examples of how to write:

Today was a nothing day, not much happened. I woke late, missed an appointment and had an argument with my mother. She's so annoying. What's the point?

OR

Slept well, work OK – short walk. Lunch with a friend – enjoyed catching up. Still haven't been to the gym but that's ok. I'll go tomorrow.

OR

Feel like I'm losing the plot. I'm so upset, had awful row with partner, it must be my fault – I can't keep my mouth shut. Want to hide under the duvet. GGRRRR.

Pay attention to significant events or interactions with others that might affect your mood. Talk about your successes, disappointments, anniversaries, illness, losses, relationships and so on.

Just before you start here are five steps to success:

1 Start each day with deep breathing (try: breathe in for four, hold for four, breathe out for four)
2 Set your intention for the day
3 Have plans in place
4 Give yourself positive affirmations
5 Write a gratitude list at the end of each day

*So, are you ready to make serious,
meaningful and positive changes in your life?
You can do it!*

DAY ONE

MOOD

FOOD & DRINK

EXERCISE

ENERGY LEVEL (from 0 to 10)

0   1   2   3   4   5   6   7   8   9   10

SLEEP

OTHER

Today I felt …

What went well?

What could have gone better?

Gratitude list:
1
2
3

My positive affirmation of the day is:

DAY TWO

MOOD

FOOD & DRINK

EXERCISE

ENERGY LEVEL (from 0 to 10)

0   1   2   3   4   5   6   7   8   9   10

SLEEP

OTHER

Today I felt …

What went well?

What could have gone better?

Gratitude list:
1
2
3

My positive affirmation of the day is:

DAY THREE

MOOD

FOOD & DRINK

EXERCISE

ENERGY LEVEL (from 0 to 10)

0   1   2   3   4   5   6   7   8   9   10

SLEEP

....

OTHER

Today I felt …

What went well?

What could have gone better?

Gratitude list:
1
2
3

My positive affirmation of the day is:

Freewriting Pages

What plays on your mind more than anything else?

_____

_____

_____

_____

_____

_____

_____

_____

Why is that a problem for you? How does it affect you?

_____

_____

_____

_____

_____

_____

_____

What can you do to change the situation, or to feel better?

What can you learn from this situation?

DAY FOUR

MOOD

FOOD & DRINK

EXERCISE

ENERGY LEVEL (from 0 to 10)

0   1   2   3   4   5   6   7   8   9   10

SLEEP

....

OTHER

Today I felt ...

What went well?

What could have gone better?

Gratitude list:
1
2
3

My positive affirmation of the day is:

DAY FIVE

MOOD

FOOD & DRINK

EXERCISE

ENERGY LEVEL (from 0 to 10)

0   1   2   3   4   5   6   7   8   9   10

SLEEP

OTHER

Today I felt ...

What went well?

What could have gone better?

Gratitude list:
1
2
3

My positive affirmation of the day is:

The Thinking Connection

Would you say that you are more of a negative or positive thinker? Is your cup half full or half empty? Does life feel difficult and challenging or exciting and stimulating? Do you make assumptions or judgements on yourself and others? Or are you a black-and-white thinker with fixed ideas?

Negative thinking can create:

* Stress, worry anxiety and panic attacks
* Sadness and depression
* Resentment, anger and jealousy
* Criticism and judgement
* Fears and phobias
* Feelings of powerlessness and hopelessness

This can lead to low energy, physical illness, insomnia and possible addictions.

Positive thinking creates:

* Peace, calm, joy and happiness
* Inspiration, motivation and determination
* Acceptance and gratitude
* Hope and opportunities

Positive thinking leads to higher energy levels and increased activity. Don't let negativity inhabit your head and steal your joy!

Many people have ANTS (automatic negative thinking system, aka NATS), which includes self-doubt, worry, self-deprecation, high expectations on yourself and others, all-or-nothing thinking, worst-case-scenario building, assumptions and judgements. Thoughts play an immensely POWERFUL role in how you feel. Be a warrior not a worrier.

Think about yourself as an Energy Bank:

Negative thinking leads to an ENERGY DEFICIT = low energy, self-doubt, depression or other physical illness.

Positive thinking leads to ENERGY CREDIT = strength, empowerment, self-belief, confidence and increased activity.

Negative thinking often involves distortions of reality and errors in thinking patterns. Don't be your biggest judge or critic! Here are eight typical negative thinking patterns. Fill in your own example of negative thinking to become more aware of how you typically relate to these thinking patterns.

THINKING PATTERN	DESCRIPTION	MY EXAMPLE	YOUR EXAMPLE
All or nothing	Looking at things in extreme, black-and-white terms	I'm not going to pass the exam, so there's no point even trying	
Assumptions	Believing that the way we feel must be true without looking at evidence that contradicts	I feel like an idiot so I must be one I won't do well in life	
Jumping to conclusions	Imagining we know what others are thinking Predicting the future	My friends think I'm boring I won't be included next time	

THINKING PATTERN	DESCRIPTION	MY EXAMPLE	YOUR EXAMPLE
Catastrophizing or minimizing	Blowing things out of proportion so the situation appears worse, or shrinking an important factor	I've got a serious health condition That lump is nothing	
Eliminating the positive	Dwelling on bad experiences and ignoring the good and positive	I messed up I always get things wrong	
Personalizing or blaming	Taking things personally, acting like a martyr/victim or not taking responsibility	It's always me – I can't do right It was their fault	
Overgeneralizing	Assuming that because something has happened once it will happen again	I tried that before and it didn't work I can't do it	

THINKING PATTERN	DESCRIPTION	MY EXAMPLE	YOUR EXAMPLE
Labelling	Giving labels to yourself and/or others	I'm disgusting He's lazy	
'Must' and 'should' thinking	Fixed expectations of how you think things should be	I must be perfect He should not have said that	

Personal growth requires an awareness of thoughts and behaviours that no longer serve you and a willingness to challenge and change them. Remember, what you give power to will have power over you.

Changing your focus from negative to positive thinking can make a huge difference to how you feel: if you find it really hard to escape your stress and anxiety and your negative thoughts are taking up way too much headspace, give yourself a break and try distracting your mind with other activities such as arts and craft projects, volunteering or hiking.

Freewriting Pages

Write down whatever comes into your head – let it go…

DAY SIX

MOOD

FOOD & DRINK

EXERCISE

ENERGY LEVEL (from 0 to 10)

0   1   2   3   4   5   6   7   8   9   10

SLEEP

. . . .

OTHER

Today I felt …

What went well?

What could have gone better?

Gratitude list:
1
2
3

My positive affirmation of the day is:

DAY SEVEN

MOOD

FOOD & DRINK

EXERCISE

ENERGY LEVEL (from 0 to 10)

0   1   2   3   4   5   6   7   8   9   10

SLEEP

OTHER

Today I felt …

What went well?

What could have gone better?

Gratitude list:
1
2
3

My positive affirmation of the day is:

Change Your Mindset Exercise

Now let's have a look at how your thinking can affect your emotions and behaviours by identifying typical negative thoughts you may have around food, exercise and sleep.

Example:

	Identify the NEGATIVE thoughts you have around the following:	Emotions	What alternative POSITIVE helpful thoughts could you have?	Emotions
Food	I can't be bothered to cook	Depressed Hopeless	I'm going to eat well today	Inspired Happy
Exercise	I hate exercise	Disappointed Weak	I'll go for a walk	Pleased Motivated
Sleep	I keep waking up at night	Anxious	I will sleep well tonight	Relaxed

Now fill in your thoughts:

	Identify the NEGATIVE thoughts you have around the following:	Emotions	What alternative POSITIVE helpful thoughts could you have?	Emotions
Food				
Exercise				
Sleep				

Week One: General Evaluation

How has the week gone for you? Have you noticed any themes running through this week?

What have been the unhelpful triggers to your moods?

What are the obstacles that stand in your way?

What are the learnings you can take forward?

Week One: Goal Planner

Think about what you could do to make next week more fun, relaxing, interesting or successful. By writing this down, you are making a written meaningful commitment to yourself.

Put the goal in your diary to ensure it happens when planned. Treat the goal as an appointment with yourself as you would any other important meeting. You are worth it!

Give yourself one realistic and achievable goal that will make a difference to how you feel.

MY GOAL FOR NEXT WEEK IS:

IT WILL HAPPEN ON (be specific about time and day(s)):

POSSIBLE OBSTACLES (if any):

I WILL OVERCOME THEM BY:

ACHIEVING THIS GOAL WILL HELP ME:

WEEK TWO

I hope the first week went well for you. Did you manage to write every day? Don't worry too much if you didn't, as all steps are progress. It can be helpful to dedicate a specific time each day to fill out your diary. Think about when will work best for you. What are you looking forward to this week? What do you hope it will bring? Have you set your goal? If not, set it now.

If completing the diary feels too hard and you feel very low or exhausted, listen to your body and get lots of rest. It is not wasting time, it's doing what is needed. Create a sacred space for yourself, surround yourself with comfortable pillows and candles and relax. Remember your positive affirmations such as:

**I am enough
I am determined**

The themed CBT worksheets for this second week focus on physical health and how exercise can improve your mental health and wellbeing. Here are some physical mood-boosting ideas:

Hiking/walking/jogging A daily walk, hike or run is a great way to practice mental and physical self-care. Walking puts you in the slow lane. It helps to burn off steam, reduce stress and gets your blood pumping. Running reduces stress, improves heart health and helps lift depression.

Cycling Burn off stress by riding a bike. It will help you feel fitter, calmer, more in control and will increase your confidence. Do you remember bike-riding as a kid and having so much fun?

Swimming Being underwater is relaxing, giving you time to switch off and meditate. Swimming as part of a regular routine will help bring structure to your week.

Gym Whether you are kickboxing, HIIT training or spinning, regular attendance at your local gym can help you feel fitter and stronger. Meet new friends, set goals to help you sleep better, gain focus and confidence.

Dancing Whether focusing on routines, such as ballet or using free flowing movements, dancing can help you feel fitter and mentally stronger. Classes bring structure and help you meet new friends and like-minded people. Developing new social bonds can open you up to other new opportunities, too.

Raise your endorphins, increase your energy level and have fun, whether it be by jogging, Tai Chi, swimming or kickboxing. It will give you an immediate boost and a sense of achievement and pride.

Do your best!

DAY ONE

MOOD

FOOD & DRINK

EXERCISE

ENERGY LEVEL (from 0 to 10)

0   1   2   3   4   5   6   7   8   9   10

SLEEP

OTHER

Today I felt ...

What went well?

What could have gone better?

Gratitude list:
1
2
3

My positive affirmation of the day is:

DAY TWO

MOOD

FOOD & DRINK

EXERCISE

ENERGY LEVEL (from 0 to 10)

0	1	2	3	4	5	6	7	8	9	10

SLEEP

OTHER

Today I felt …

What went well?

What could have gone better?

Gratitude list:

1

2

3

My positive affirmation of the day is:

DAY THREE

MOOD

FOOD & DRINK

EXERCISE

ENERGY LEVEL (from 0 to 10)

0   1   2   3   4   5   6   7   8   9   10

SLEEP

OTHER

Today I felt …

What went well?

What could have gone better?

Gratitude list:
1
2
3

My positive affirmation of the day is:

Freewriting Pages

What would you like to think about this week?

_____

_____

_____

_____

_____

_____

_____

_____

Would you like anything to change? If so, what and why?

_____

_____

_____

_____

_____

_____

_____

_____

What can you do about it?

How will that make you feel better?

DAY FOUR

MOOD

FOOD & DRINK

EXERCISE

ENERGY LEVEL (from 0 to 10)

0   1   2   3   4   5   6   7   8   9   10

SLEEP

OTHER

Today I felt …

What went well?

What could have gone better?

Gratitude list:
1
2
3

My positive affirmation of the day is:

DAY FIVE

MOOD

FOOD & DRINK

EXERCISE

ENERGY LEVEL (from 0 to 10)

0   1   2   3   4   5   6   7   8   9   10

SLEEP

OTHER

Today I felt …

What went well?

What could have gone better?

Gratitude list:
1
2
3

My positive affirmation of the day is:

The Exercise Connection

It's easy to get into bad habits but just as easy to break them. How many times have you joined a gym and not bothered to go?

Lack of physical activity:

* Prolongs depression
* Can lead to weight gain and other more serious health conditions

Increased physical activity:

* Increases stamina and resilience
* Gives mental focus, which can promote productivity and creativity
* Takes attention away from anxiety, obsessions, worries and conflict
* Develops a positive mental attitude
* Provides opportunities to meet new people and make friends
* Helps to bring routine and structure to your week

You can start slow with small, achievable goals that you build up over a period of time and can include many options such as walking, hiking, swimming, football, rugby, dancing, yoga or even parkour, if you fancy jumping over buildings! OK, I'm not expecting you to go that far, at least for now. Exercise in fresh air will doubly increase your feelgood factor.

Exercise is not a fad or a quick fix, it's a lifestyle change that takes time to develop until it becomes second nature. How early do you start your day? Becoming a morning person could give you an energy boost for the day and help you sleep better.

Don't let negative thinking be an obstacle.

TYPICAL NEGATIVE THOUGHTS	ALTERNATIVE POSITIVE THOUGHTS
I haven't got time	I'll make time
I'm not fit enough	I'm going to get fitter
I won't look good at the gym	I'm going to get in shape
I'm useless at exercise	I'll start with walking

Now fill in your thoughts:

Freewriting Pages

Write down whatever comes into your head – let it go…

DAY SIX

MOOD

FOOD & DRINK

EXERCISE

ENERGY LEVEL (from 0 to 10)

0	1	2	3	4	5	6	7	8	9	10

SLEEP

OTHER

Today I felt …

What went well?

What could have gone better?

Gratitude list:
1
2
3

My positive affirmation of the day is:

DAY SEVEN

MOOD

FOOD & DRINK

EXERCISE

ENERGY LEVEL (from 0 to 10)

0   1   2   3   4   5   6   7   8   9   10

SLEEP

....

OTHER

Today I felt ...

What went well?

What could have gone better?

Gratitude list:
1
2
3

My positive affirmation of the day is:

The Physical Health Connection

People affected by health difficulties sometimes also have perfectionist tendencies, which prolongs recovery. Being hard on yourself or expecting too much too soon can lead to fear of trying even the small steps. When you tell yourself that something will be too much for you, you create an obstacle in your mind. This might be due to worrying about disappointing yourself or others or failing in some way, or being concerned about the recovery itself and what that might entail. Perhaps you have lost confidence in who you are and what you can achieve. Living life behind a barrier is not a life you deserve. Find nourishment for the soul.

Things to try:

* Making a plan
* Setting achievable goals
* Finding joy in fun and interesting activities
* Starting with gentle exercise and then building up
* Spending time in nature
* Self-compassion and kindness
* Being okay with being okay

Example of negative thinking

SITUATION	TYPICAL NEGATIVE THOUGHTS	ALTERNATIVE POSITIVE THOUGHTS
Being invited to a festival	I might get worse	This might help me to feel better
	I'm not strong enough	I'll take it slow
	I might need the toilet	I'll find the toilets
	I'll look out of place	I'll be fine

Here is a CBT worksheet for you to explore any negative thoughts you have around your health.

SITUATION	NEGATIVE THOUGHTS Strength of belief (1–100%)	NEGATIVE EMOTIONS Intensity of emotion (1–100%)

SAME SITUATION	POSITIVE THOUGHTS Strength of belief (1–100%)	POSITIVE EMOTIONS Intensity of emotion (1–100%)

Week Two: General Evaluation

What have you noticed this week? What has gone well?

What was your biggest challenge? How did you overcome it?

If you achieved your goal, how has it helped? Or if you didn't, why?

What does this tell you about yourself?

Week Two: Goal Planner

If last week's goal worked for you, keep it going and add another goal for next week.

I WILL CONTINUE WITH:

Give yourself a realistic and achievable goal that will make a difference to how you feel.

MY GOAL FOR NEXT WEEK IS:

IT WILL HAPPEN ON (be specific about time and day(s)):

POSSIBLE OBSTACLES (if any):

I WILL OVERCOME THEM BY:

ACHIEVING THIS GOAL WILL HELP ME:

WEEK THREE

You are now about to enter week three and by now you will hopefully have noticed some significant changes in your moods, emotions and lifestyle. If you have been following the plan, writing things out and achieving the goals, but are still feeling low, you may be experiencing depression, in which case it can take a while longer before you feel the difference. There is something to learn in everything we do, so keep going and be extra kind to yourself because you are worth it. Talk to others: a GP or friends and family. You are not alone!

Do find a regular time to write your diary and be as honest as you can; it is yours to keep, and one day in the future, you can look back and remember this period of your life as a time of transition, recovery, learning and healing. Most people become depressed and unwell because of a stressful incident or series of incidents or because life just isn't meeting their needs. What do you need to feel better?

To feel better I need (write it down):

How much of what you wrote down is possible or achievable? Are you waiting on others, or situations to change? If so, you could be waiting a long time. Life can be within your control, but in order to gain control and stop personal suffering you might need to let go of anger, expectations, situations and/or other people. Change can be very hard because it is sometimes easier to sit in familiarity rather than stepping out of your comfort zone. Make a choice, take a chance and see the change.

The themed CBT worksheets for this third week focus on our relationship to food and sleep. Being more thoughtful about what we eat can have have a positive impact on our moods, as can a good night's rest.

HEALTHY EATING TIPS:

* Start your day well by eating breakfast – skipping meals can lead to mood slumps
* Eat slow-release energy food such as pasta, rice, wholegrain breads, nuts, seeds and oats (avoid white unrefined where possible)
* Cut down on sugar
* Boost your brain – oily fish, walnuts, avocados, milk, cheese, eggs and olive and sunflower oils
* Eat slowly; take your time to enjoy
* Have an attitude of gratitude and be mindful of tastes and smells
* Drink lots of water to stay hydrated

SLEEP TIPS:

* Stick to a strict schedule of bedtime and wake times to reset your body clock (your circadian rhythm)
* Have a bedtime ritual, such as a warm bath or a milky drink
* Make your bedroom a peaceful, relaxing place: remove clutter; spray lavender on your pillow
* Exercise regularly so your body welcomes sleep
* Avoid blue light from phones or laptops for at least one hour before bedtime (it will trick your brain into thinking it's daytime)
* Always write your to-do list before 8pm

DAY ONE

MOOD

FOOD & DRINK

EXERCISE

ENERGY LEVEL (from 0 to 10)

0   1   2   3   4   5   6   7   8   9   10

SLEEP

OTHER

Today I felt ...

What went well?

What could have gone better?

Gratitude list:
1
2
3

My positive affirmation of the day is:

DAY TWO

MOOD

FOOD & DRINK

EXERCISE

ENERGY LEVEL (from 0 to 10)

0   1   2   3   4   5   6   7   8   9   10

SLEEP

OTHER

Today I felt …

What went well?

What could have gone better?

Gratitude list:

1

2

3

My positive affirmation of the day is:

DAY THREE

MOOD

FOOD & DRINK

EXERCISE

ENERGY LEVEL (from 0 to 10)

0   1   2   3   4   5   6   7   8   9   10

SLEEP

_____

OTHER

Today I felt …

What went well?

What could have gone better?

Gratitude list:
1
2
3

My positive affirmation of the day is:

Freewriting Pages

Describe yourself and your life:

What are your skills and talents?

What are your personal qualities?

What are your top five memories: the highest points in your life,
the times when you felt most alive and happy?

DAY FOUR

MOOD

FOOD & DRINK

EXERCISE

ENERGY LEVEL (from 0 to 10)

| 0 | 1 | 2 | 3 | 4 | 5 | 6 | 7 | 8 | 9 | 10 |

SLEEP

OTHER

Today I felt ...

What went well?

What could have gone better?

Gratitude list:
1
2
3

My positive affirmation of the day is:

DAY FIVE

MOOD

FOOD & DRINK

EXERCISE

ENERGY LEVEL (from 0 to 10)

| 0 | 1 | 2 | 3 | 4 | 5 | 6 | 7 | 8 | 9 | 10 |

SLEEP

OTHER

Today I felt …

What went well?

What could have gone better?

Gratitude list:
1
2
3

My positive affirmation of the day is:

The Sleep Connection

What is a good night's sleep?

Falling asleep within 15–20 minutes of your head touching the pillow, and regularly getting a total of 7–9 hours of uninterrupted sleep and waking up feeling refreshed. Not lying awake in the night, checking your phone and worrying about getting back to sleep.

What happens during sleep?

The body goes through a cycle of sleep stages from light sleep to deeper REM sleep, where most dreams happen. A good sleep re-energizes cells, clears the mind, supports memory and learning, fights illness and disease and promotes healing.

Dreaming

Freud, the father of psychology, talked about our dreams being 'the royal road to our unconscious' and dream interpretation as a way to understand human experience. Dreams can also be seen as the theatre of our unresolved issues, which can help us see what needs to be addressed. If you feel fear in a dream, then perhaps fear is what you need to overcome. Alternatively, if you feel trapped in a dream, then maybe it's time for a change. Dream interpretation is an interesting way to make sense of your life.

Examples of thoughts around sleep

SITUATION	TYPICAL NEGATIVE THOUGHTS	ALTERNATIVE POSITIVE THOUGHTS
Going to sleep	Here we go again	My body is so tired
	I never sleep well	I'm ready to rest
	I've got too much to think about	My to-do list is done – I can let go

Now try filling in a CBT worksheet looking at any situation that stops you having a good night's sleep.

SITUATION	NEGATIVE THOUGHTS Strength of belief (1–100%)	NEGATIVE EMOTIONS Intensity of emotion (1–100%)

SAME SITUATION	POSITIVE THOUGHTS Strength of belief (1–100%)	POSITIVE EMOTIONS Intensity of emotion (1–100%)

Freewriting Pages

Write down whatever comes into your head – let it go…

DAY SIX

MOOD

FOOD & DRINK

EXERCISE

ENERGY LEVEL (from 0 to 10)

0   1   2   3   4   5   6   7   8   9   10

SLEEP

OTHER

Today I felt ...

What went well?

What could have gone better?

Gratitude list:

1

2

3

My positive affirmation of the day is:

DAY SEVEN

MOOD

FOOD & DRINK

EXERCISE

ENERGY LEVEL (from 0 to 10)

0	1	2	3	4	5	6	7	8	9	10

SLEEP

OTHER

Today I felt …

What went well?

What could have gone better?

Gratitude list:
1
2
3

My positive affirmation of the day is:

The Food Connection

What is your relationship like with food? Are you an emotional eater, reaching for the biscuit tin when you feel down? Do you struggle with weight issues? Perhaps you are a binge eater or don't eat enough. Maybe you throw up after eating or restrict calories even though others tell you that you are underweight.

Poor nutrition is:

* Processed food, junk food, takeaways, fried food (saturated fats)
* Too much sugary food like cakes, biscuits, chocolates and drinks
* Too much caffeine: found in coffee, chocolate and energy drinks, it can cause anxiety and sleep issues
* Excess alcohol, which leads to anxiety, depression and sleep problems and, in alcoholics, can lead to malnutrition
* Eating either too much or not enough

Good nutrition includes:

* Eating a balanced nutritious diet
* Wholefoods, lentils, beans, pulses, nuts, seeds, brown rice, oats, quinoa,
* Five or more servings of fresh fruit and vegetables a day
* Lean protein
* Sufficient carbohydrates, fats, protein, calcium and foods rich in vitamins and minerals
* Limited amounts of salt, saturated fat and added sugar

Poor nutrition leads to:

* Being overweight or underweight
* Illness and disease
* Lower energy levels
* Negative self-talk – guilt, regret and recrimination

Good nutrition leads to:

* Positive mental and physical health
* Higher energy levels
* Motivation and self-worth
* More focus and responsibility for self-care and self-healing

Med-sense

Be sensible about what you eat if you are on medication. Look carefully at labels and warning signs to avoid foods and drinks that could have side effects.

Now try filling in a CBT worksheet looking at your thoughts and beliefs around food, eating or body image.

SITUATION	NEGATIVE THOUGHTS Strength of belief (1–100%)	NEGATIVE EMOTIONS Intensity of emotion (1–100%)

SAME SITUATION	POSITIVE THOUGHTS Strength of belief (1–100%)	POSITIVE EMOTIONS Intensity of emotion (1–100%)

Week Three: General Evaluation

How have your moods and emotions been this week?

What has influenced the way you have felt?

What efforts are you making to be conscious of exercise and nutrition? What changes and benefits are you experiencing?

If you are not doing as well as you hoped, what is holding you back?

Week Three: Goal Planner

If you have found success with your previous goals keep them going. In addition, think of an enjoyable activity to add as your new goal for this week:

I WILL CONTINUE WITH:

Give yourself a realistic and achievable goal that will make a difference to how you feel.

MY GOAL FOR NEXT WEEK IS:

IT WILL HAPPEN ON (be specific about time and day(s)):

POSSIBLE OBSTACLES (if any):

I WILL OVERCOME THEM BY:

THIS ACTIVITY WILL HELP ME:

WEEK FOUR

I sincerely hope you are feeling the benefits of this process and feeling far more in control of your life. The exercises, tips and guidance in this diary are there to support you on your journey to wellness. We are all 'works in progress' when it comes to self-knowledge.

As a therapist, however, I understand that some people are more self-motivated than others and some people want to be self-motivated but just can't seem to get going. When it comes to mental health challenges, it's always good to talk to others for support and feedback. If you are still struggling, then I fully encourage you to talk to a friend, family member or to a professional who will know how to help you. While CBT is a tried and tested solution-focused approach to mood management it is not for everyone. For some, a listening ear, empathy and compassion are far more beneficial. You have a story and it needs telling.

For those of you that are steaming ahead, think about what else you can do to enrich your life even further. How do you want to see yourself in five years' time? Nothing much will change without you making it happen.

Is furthering your education an option? Read about what's on offer at your local college or university. Maybe travel is the answer – take time out of your life to learn more about the world and other cultures. Use the space below to write down some ideas.

To move forward I will (write it down):

The themed CBT worksheets for this final week focus on relationships and self-esteem. Problems in relationships that affect moods and emotional wellbeing are:

* Poor communication
* Conflict
* Abuse
* Betrayal
* Addiction
* Break-ups
* Lack of trust

Use the worksheets to write down your thoughts and emotions on conflicts in any of your relationships to help you understand yourself. Pay particular attention to your affirmations this week while you focus on your self-esteem. Some examples of affirmations for self-care are:

I am unique
I can ask for what I need
I am enough
I don't need to be perfect
I am ME

DAY ONE

MOOD

FOOD & DRINK

EXERCISE

ENERGY LEVEL (from 0 to 10)

| 0 | 1 | 2 | 3 | 4 | 5 | 6 | 7 | 8 | 9 | 10 |

SLEEP

....

OTHER

Today I felt …

What went well?

What could have gone better?

Gratitude list:
1
2
3

My positive affirmation of the day is:

DAY TWO

MOOD

FOOD & DRINK

EXERCISE

ENERGY LEVEL (from 0 to 10)

| 0 | 1 | 2 | 3 | 4 | 5 | 6 | 7 | 8 | 9 | 10 |

SLEEP

....

OTHER

Today I felt …

What went well?

What could have gone better?

Gratitude list:
1
2
3

My positive affirmation of the day is:

DAY THREE

MOOD

FOOD & DRINK

EXERCISE

ENERGY LEVEL (from 0 to 10)

| 0 | 1 | 2 | 3 | 4 | 5 | 6 | 7 | 8 | 9 | 10 |

SLEEP

....

OTHER

Today I felt …

What went well?

What could have gone better?

Gratitude list:

1

2

3

My positive affirmation of the day is:

Freewriting Pages

Write about any unresolved issues involving love and/or a relationship that need to be let go of.

What was the situation?

_____

_____

_____

_____

_____

_____

_____

_____

What did that mean to you? How do you feel about it now?

_____

_____

_____

_____

_____

_____

_____

Are there any other perspectives that you might have?

What needs to happen for you to move forward?

DAY FOUR

MOOD

FOOD & DRINK

EXERCISE

ENERGY LEVEL (from 0 to 10)

| 0 | 1 | 2 | 3 | 4 | 5 | 6 | 7 | 8 | 9 | 10 |

SLEEP

··

OTHER

Today I felt …

What went well?

What could have gone better?

Gratitude list:
1
2
3

My positive affirmation of the day is:

DAY FIVE

MOOD

FOOD & DRINK

EXERCISE

ENERGY LEVEL (from 0 to 10)

| 0 | 1 | 2 | 3 | 4 | 5 | 6 | 7 | 8 | 9 | 10 |

SLEEP

....

OTHER

Today I felt …

What went well?

What could have gone better?

Gratitude list:

1

2

3

My positive affirmation of the day is:

The Love and Relationship Connection

Falling in love can feel like a wonderful high, yet at the same time overwhelming and hard to handle, especially in the early days of a relationship. How do the relationships in your life affect your emotions? How quickly do you fall in or out of love? Do your relationships feel secure or insecure? Are you repeating negative patterns? Some people know what they are looking for and will have a good, clear sense of whether a potential partner meets their needs. They will know when to walk away. Others are not so clear, are happy or even grateful for attention and do not heed warning signs when things start to feel wrong. Good relationships require both people to communicate well, and to make an effort to build shared future dreams based on love and respect.

Positive friendships are also important for emotional wellbeing. Your friends need to have your back and vice versa. Good relationships help you feel secure and trusting, rather than jealous, over-competitive or subjecting yourself to negative peer pressure. If you constantly worry about friendship groups, then maybe it's time to step back and evaluate. It might be as simple as speaking up for yourself or even knowing when to walk away.

Let's look at relationships using the CBT approach. Think of any situation that has bothered you that involved either a partner or someone close. This could be a conflict situation or one where you have had bad feelings about yourself.

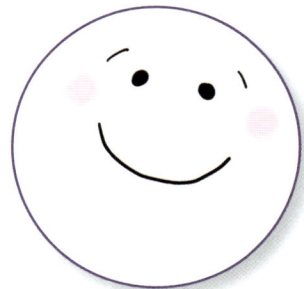

SITUATION	NEGATIVE THOUGHTS Strength of belief (1–100%)	NEGATIVE EMOTIONS Intensity of emotion (1–100%)

SAME SITUATION	POSITIVE THOUGHTS Strength of belief (1–100%)	POSITIVE EMOTIONS Intensity of emotion (1–100%)

Freewriting Pages

Who has been the greatest inspiration in your life and why?

What can you learn from this person?

In what ways could you inspire others?

How could you make that happen?

DAY SIX

MOOD

FOOD & DRINK

EXERCISE

ENERGY LEVEL (from 0 to 10)

0   1   2   3   4   5   6   7   8   9   10

SLEEP

....

OTHER

Today I felt …

What went well?

What could have gone better?

Gratitude list:
1
2
3

My positive affirmation of the day is:

DAY SEVEN

MOOD

FOOD & DRINK

EXERCISE

ENERGY LEVEL (from 0 to 10)

0	1	2	3	4	5	6	7	8	9	10

SLEEP

....

OTHER

Today I felt …

What went well?

What could have gone better?

Gratitude list:
1
2
3

My positive affirmation of the day is:

The Self-Esteem Connection

Now let's look at confidence and self-esteem. Think of a specific situation that has worried you. This could be an example taken from work, school, family or friendships. Write down your thoughts and emotions about this situation in the CBT worksheet on the opposite page.

Keep going with these sheets, even after the diary has finished. It can take many weeks to retrain your brain. Make your own sheets for the future.

Examples of thinking around self-esteem

SITUATION	TYPICAL NEGATIVE THOUGHTS	ALTERNATIVE POSITIVE THOUGHTS
Taking on a new project at work	I'll mess up	This is a learning opportunity
	I'll make a fool of myself	I worked hard to get here
	I can't do it	I'll do it

SITUATION	NEGATIVE THOUGHTS Strength of belief (1–100%)	NEGATIVE EMOTIONS Intensity of emotion (1–100%)

SAME SITUATION	POSITIVE THOUGHTS Strength of belief (1–100%)	POSITIVE EMOTIONS Intensity of emotion (1–100%)

Week Four: General Evaluation

How was this week? List the highs and the lows:

List three of your best coping strategies.

What were you most grateful for this week?

List the positive affirmations that work best for you.

Week Four: Goal Planner

If you have found success with your previous goals keep them going. In addition think of enjoyable activities to add to the list:

ACTIVITIES I WILL CONTINUE:

OTHER IDEAS FOR ACTIVITIES:

WHAT I NEED TO DO TO STAY FOCUSED AND MAINTAIN MY NEW ROUTINE:

POSSIBLE OBSTACLES (if any):

I WILL OVERCOME THEM BY:

THESE ACTIVITIES WILL HELP ME:

Final Evaluation

Overall how has completing this diary helped you?

What were your most useful strategies for mood management?

What did you find hard (if anything) and why?

What were the most powerful changes you made and why?

Write down three new positive actions for the future:

How do you see your life going forward now?

Conclusion

It has been a pleasure to have been part of this diary journey with you for the past 4 weeks. Whatever you have learned will now be embedded deep within you for the future. Lifelong habits can be broken in a short time and there is no reason why you need to ever pick them up again. Some people worry that change won't last, that it is temporary and that things will go back if something bad happens. However, you need not worry at all – worrying doesn't help or change things. Instead, read and reread the tips, ideas and strategies in this diary and keep up the healthy lifestyle changes you have made.

So for now, it's goodbye and I wish you all the very best for future success on your journey to wellness.

Much love

Andrea ♡

DON'T FORGET:

▶ There is no time limit on recovery.

▶ Meditation and mindfulness – be in the moment.

▶ Check your thinking using the CBT model.

▶ Distract from anxiety to change your focus in a positive way.

▶ Listen to yourself – you know what's best for you.

▶ Let go of perfectionism.

▶ Stop comparing yourself – there is only one beautiful, unique you.

▶ Encourage yourself and value yourself – use positive affirmations.

▶ Talk it out – you are not alone.

▶ Accept and forgive yourself and others – we are only human.

▶ Give hugs, love and affection – they are so healing!

Don't forget to check out my card decks, other books, products and resources for mental health: *The Mood Cards, Understand Deep Emotions* and *The Mood Book*.

To find out more about me and the way I work, please take a look at my websites, where I have well over 100 articles on a variety of topics:

www.themoodcards.com

www.andreaharrn.co.uk

Connect with me:
Twitter @themoodcards or @moodcards
Instagram @themoodcards
LinkedIn or Facebook at Andrea Harrn Psychotherapist

Your Notes

Continue to use CBT worksheets to rewire your brain and write about your thoughts and emotions.

SITUATION	NEGATIVE THOUGHTS Strength of belief (1–100%)	NEGATIVE EMOTIONS Intensity of emotion (1–100%)

SAME SITUATION	POSITIVE THOUGHTS Strength of belief (1–100%)	POSITIVE EMOTIONS Intensity of emotion (1–100%)

SITUATION	NEGATIVE THOUGHTS Strength of belief (1–100%)	NEGATIVE EMOTIONS Intensity of emotion (1–100%)

SAME SITUATION	POSITIVE THOUGHTS Strength of belief (1–100%)	POSITIVE EMOTIONS Intensity of emotion (1–100%)

Acknowledgements

There are so many amazing, clever, inspirational writers, thinkers, philosophers, psychologists, counsellors, psychotherapists, life coaches, artists, musicians, poets, professors at UEL, workshop leaders, teachers, thought leaders, spiritual and religious texts that have influenced my work as a therapist and a writer. All have played a huge part in shaping me, helping me to understand myself, be the best version of myself and accept the times I fall way below my own standards. You have helped me understand what it means to be human and how to bring that humanity, with loving kindness, into the world.

For putting this diary into production: Thank you to everyone at Eddison Books, particularly, Lisa Dyer, Nicolette Kaponis and Braz Atkins for your patience and expert skills. Massive thanks to Severine Jeauneau for ongoing belief and support in all The Mood Card products and exceptional worldwide sales in such a short time. It is humbling to think that thousands of people from Australia, to USA through Europe and the Far East have the cards and books and I have every confidence that this diary will reach those who can benefit. You are all amazing!!!!

Thank you to Nick Eddison for believing in The Mood Cards from that very first meeting at the London Book Fair back in 2014. Although you are no longer at Eddison Books, hopefully you are enjoying your retirement on an exotic beach somewhere or walking in nature around the UK. You are still much appreciated for all the early help and support you gave me as a new author.

To my agent Sandy Violette at the Abner Stein agency. You help me in so many ways. I feel very blessed to have you if my life and on my side. Your agency works with so many awesome incredible well-known authors. I still remember that first time you saw the mock-up of the Mood Cards in that café in Kensington and you offered to be my agent. You saw the power of the work I am doing to help people with mental health issues. I could not have got this far without your many years of professional experience, your kind and patient approach and your belief in me.

To Stacey Siddons, your gorgeous little faces continue to help others. You are a very talented lady and I am so lucky to have met you, all those years ago. Love, thanks and appreciation once again for all your amazing art and design work and help in general where needed.

To Melissa June Hobbs. Lots of love and gratitude for your continuing support, research and energy into The Mood Card Project.

To my dear parents, Helena and David Hockley who have always been on my side. Dad, you left this world nearly 30 years ago but I still feel your calm energy within me. Thank you for your wicked sense of humour, teaching me to take risks, show steel and believe in myself. Thank you Mum for all your support, teaching me manners, morals, duty and the importance of family. To my dear sisters: I feel truly blessed. Bev: always there for me when needed, which is quite often! You are the most kind, generous, thoughtful, caring and supportive sister anyone could every wish for. Diane: a very special sister and much loved. You taught me empathy and compassion and will always remain deeply embedded in my heart.

To my dear husband Andrew. Thanks for being my rock, my shoulder and the person I know I can rely on. The Keeper of the Castle and the Fixer of all that breaks, including me! I am truly blessed to have you in my life.

To my grown-up children Alex, Victoria and Ben. I am so proud of each and every one of you. Thank you for always supporting me and showing interest in my work and my life and thank you for the gift of grandchildren, Oilibhéar, Theo and Levi Blue who bring love, light and joy into our lives. We have many days to look forward to and many memories to make.

Thank you also to my amazing extended family, friends and work colleagues for being such an important part of my life. We share our lives, through good and bad and I'm grateful for each and every one of you. Special thanks to Tom, Kerri, Mathilde, Paul, Jon, Talia, Tash, Lee, Rosie, Mark, Nick, Paul, Marilyn, Jill, David, Linda, Harvey, Verna, Richard, Carol, Malcolm, Ruth, Richard, Carol, Gordon, Toni, Barb, Sandy, Odette, Debs, Amelia, Deanna, Beverly and Stanford, Sandra, Jeff, Roz and Adi, Terri and Mark (this is not an exhaustive list of those I love and appreciate). We are there for each other.

A huge thank you to everyone else that has been there for me over the past year or so, giving encouragement, love, support, feedback, time, wisdom and practical support. Specifically a HUGE thank you to my Facebook and Twitter community who have readily engaged in all sorts of random conversations about mental health and have really helped me get my thoughts in order. You are loved and valued xx.

Lastly and by no means least, my biggest thanks has to go to all my clients over the past 20 years who have shared their lives with me in my therapy room, allowed me to join them in their worlds and understand life from so many different perspectives, cultures and view points. It has been my sincere pleasure to have met you all and worked with you as your therapist. I feel humbled and honoured to have been part of your journey and I wish you all the peace, happiness and love that you deserve.

Much love to you all

Andrea ♡

Resources

Books

Dupont, Caroline Marie, *Enlightened Eating*. Alive Books, 2006.

Greenberger, Dennis, Padesky, Christine A., *Mind Over Mood*. New York: Gilford Press, 1995.

Healy, Maureen (ed), *My Mixed Emotions*. London: DK Children, 2018.

Holford, Patrick, *Optimum Nutrition for the Mind*. London: Piatkus, 2007.

Hyman, Bruce M., Pedrick, Cherry, *The OCD Workbook (2nd edition)*. Oakland: New Harbinger Publications, 2005.

Medina, John, *Brain Rules*. Seatle: Pear Press, 2008.

Reader's Digest, *Foods that Harm, Foods that Heal*, New York: Reader's Digest, 2002.

Online

www.wikipedia.org

www.centreformentalhealth.org.uk

EDDISON BOOKS LIMITED

Managing Director Lisa Dyer

Managing Editor Nicolette Kaponis

Editor Claire Rogers

Designer Brazzle Atkins

Proofreader Nicola Hodgson

Production Gary Hayes